Dorm Dining 101

To order additional copies, please contact us.
BookSurge, LLC
www.booksurge.com
1-866-308-6235
orders@booksurge.com

FRESHLY PREPARED BY,
LEE BAKER

DORM
DINING 101

YOUR GUIDE TO EASY,
CHEAP AND LOW
MAINTENANCE COOKING
FOR THE UNIVERSITY
STUDENT

2004

Dorm Dining 101

TABLE OF CONTENTS

This Book Was Inspired By My Daughter Katy Who Is Heading Off To University. These Recipes Are From Our Family, Friends And Our Own Kitchen. Special Thanks to Kym and her editing prowess.

STOCKING THE PANTRY

There is nothing worse than starting to cook something to eat or you get a craving for something special and you don't have all the ingredients. I have put a list together of mostly what you will need to make these recipes. I did not include a lot of the fresh meats or fresh vegetables as you can get those along the way.

Raiding your parents spice cupboard is highly recommended. Put a bunch of spices and herbs in some baggies and label them. This way you have more variety. I've included minimal spices in these recipes so you don't need a whole selection. *Tip*: instead of needing basil and oregano, just get Italian seasoning.

As for measurements, use your 250 ml can, fill it with water and poor it in a mug. That will be your benchmark from then on. As for teaspoons and tablespoons, nothing is iron clad. Use your kitchen utensils. Pinches and handfuls work just fine if you don't have measuring spoons and measuring cups. Improvise! Create your own flavours.

These recipes don't need to be an exact science. As long as you have a balanced ratio you will do just fine.

Tip: you can use cups, mugs, glasses and regular spoons for your measuring requirements.

Spices & Herbs

Italian seasoning
Pepper
Salt
Cajun seasoning
Hot sauce
Paprika
Chicken bouillon powder

Canned Goods

Salmon
Tuna
Pork & beans
Tomato sauce
Tomato paste
Sliced potatoes
Cream of mushroom soup
Cream of chicken soup
Dijon mustard
Plum tomatoes
Mushrooms
Chicken broth
Beef broth

Miscellaneous

Peanut butter
Cheese whiz
Butter or margarine
Eggs
Minced garlic in oil
Parmesan cheese
Italian salad dressing
Mayonnaise
Carrots
Potatoes
Onions
Vegetable oil
Breadcrumbs
Corn Starch
Olive oil
Brown sugar
Ketchup
HP Sauce
Balsamic vinegar
Worchester sauce
Non-stick vegetable spray
Soya sauce
Sugar
White flour
Bisquick
White vinegar

Pasta & Rice

Spaghetti noodles
Converted rice
Penne

APPETIZERS

Artichoke Dip

1 cup mayonnaise
1 can artichokes
1 cup parmesan cheese

Drain and chop artichokes. In an oven proof dish add mayo, artichokes and cheese and stir well to combine. Put in oven at 350° or in microwave for about 5 minutes or until cheese is melted and heated through. Serve with Triscuits.

Spinach or Veggie Dip

1 500 ml. container sour cream
1 cup mayonnaise
1 pkg Knorr spinach or vegetable soup mix
1 round loaf of pumpernickel or sour dough bread

Cut top off bread and hollow out the middle to make a bowl. Reserve the bread for later use. In the meantime mix all ingredients together and let stand several hours or overnight. Poor mixture into bread bowl and use the pulled bread to dip into the mixture. Or if you prefer omit the bread all together and just make the dip and use crackers.

Gramy's Garlic Bread

1 fresh baguette
½ cup melted butter
2 cloves garlic minced
2 tbs parmesan cheese (optional)

Slice baguette in thin slices and place on baking sheet. Add garlic to butter and poor evenly over bread. Sprinkle with Parmesan and broil until toasted. About 5 minutes. Watch carefully.

Bruschetta

3 large tomatoes
2 tsp. garlic minced
2 tsp salt
4 tbs olive oil
1 Baguette sliced

Dice tomatoes and put them in a bowl along with garlic, salt and oil. Toss. Let sit about ½ hour to allow flavours to blend. Serve with sliced baguette.

EGGS AND CHEESE

Hardboiled Eggs

In saucepan large enough to hold eggs, add water to cover your eggs. Boil eggs over medium high heat for 8-12 minutes from the time of boiling. Remove from heat and run under cold water to set.

Egg Salad

2 hardboiled eggs chopped
salt and pepper to taste
1 green onion finely chopped
1 tbs mayonnaise

Mix all ingredients together. Season to taste. If dry add more mayonnaise.

Soft-boiled Eggs

In boiling water gently add egg with a spoon being careful not to drop heavily into pot. Set timer for about 4 minutes. Remove from pot and run under cold water to stop cooking process.

Eggs To Go

1 english muffin
1 egg
slice of cold cut i.e.: ham, turkey
slice of cheese or cheese whiz

While toasting english muffin, spray non-stick spray in small microwave bowl. Crack one egg and microwave 30-50 seconds until cooked. Put cheese and meat on english muffin and place egg on top. Voila!

Scrambled Eggs

Done in the microwave they take on a soufflé like texture

In microwave proof bowl spray cooking spray. Add two eggs and whisk with fork adding a teaspoon of water. Place in microwave until puffy about 40 seconds to 1 minute.

Cheesy Scrambled Eggs

Same as above except omit water and add 2 tablespoons of cheese whiz.

Easy Cheese Sauce

2 tbs butter or margarine
1 tbs flour
1/2 cup milk
4 tbs Cheese whiz

Melt butter in saucepan add flour and stir until a paste is made. Add milk and bring to a boil until thickened stirring constantly. Add cheese whiz. Lower heat. Mix well. Use over english muffins, eggs or just over toast as "Welsh Rabbit".

Welsh Rabbit

There is an ongoing debate over "Welsh Rabbit" or Welsh Rarebit". The story goes that in the old days when the men came back empty handed after a day of hunting they had to resort to eating melted cheese on bread. They had a "rare" bit of food, or it was mock "rabbit".

Simply prepare cheese sauce (above) and poor over toast.

SALADS

French Salad

This may look complicated but it is full of protein, fibre and well worth the effort.

1/2 head lettuce
2 hard-boiled eggs (see recipe page 5)
1 can oil packed, drained tuna
6 black olives (optional)
1 boiled potato peeled and cut into pieces
handful of steamed green beans chilled
salt & pepper to taste
1/2 can of anchovy fillets
1 tomato thinly sliced
2 green onions chopped
¼ cup Italian dressing

Add all ingredients except lettuce, eggs and tuna. Toss with Italian vinaigrette. Let stand 10 minutes. Add lettuce. Toss again. Then add tuna and eggs arranging on salad top. Season again to taste. Add more dressing if desired. Serves 2.

Mediterranean Salad

2 large, ripe tomatoes sliced

½ container of feta cheese, drained and sliced or crumbled
1 tbs Italian herb seasoning (fresh is always best but expensive)
¼ cup Italian dressing
salt and pepper to taste

On a large plate alternate slices of tomato and feta. Sprinkle with dried basil. Drizzle dressing all over. Season with salt and pepper. Let stand 5 minutes to allow basil flavour to permeate the tomato.

Pasta Salad

½ bag of penne, rigatoni or fusilli pasta
2 green onions chopped
½ cucumber peeled chopped *
1 container feta cheese crumbled
¼ cup of mayonnaise
1 green pepper chopped
salt and pepper
2 tbs Italian dressing
1 tsp dried basil or oregano or Italian seasoning

Cook pasta until Al Dente**. Rinse under cold water in colander until cool. Combine all ingredients in large bowl with pasta and mix well. Season and adjust mayonnaise and dressing. Note: pasta salad is best if left for a while in fridge for flavours to merge together. But you can also eat it right away. Makes excellent leftover lunch so make lots.

* English cucumber is more expensive, but you don't need to peel it. If you get the regular, fatter cucumber you need to peel the skin.

** Al Dente-firm not mushy

Potato Salad

2 hard-boiled eggs, peeled
3 Yukon gold potatoes
salt and pepper
½ cup mayonnaise
¼ cup light sour cream
1 tsp Dijon mustard or ½ tsp powdered mustard
2 green onions chopped
1 tsp paprika

Boil potatoes until tender and let cool completely in fridge. Peel 2 of the 3 potatoes. Chop all 3 potatoes into 1-inch cubes, including the skin of the 3rd potato. In large bowl add potatoes and all other ingredients. Mix well. Adjust seasoning. Refrigerate for 1 hour to let flavours blend.

DINNERS

Chicken Italiano

This is done entirely in the microwave

1 medium onion, sliced
½ cup of celery chopped
1 clove garlic, minced
1 tbs butter or margarine
1 tbs cornstarch
1/3 cup water
2/3 cup ketchup
¼ tsp salt and pepper
dash of dried basil leaves
dash of dried thyme leaves
1 lb skinless boneless chicken breasts or thighs cut into
1-inch cubes
4 cups hot cooked pasta

Place onion, celery, garlic and butter in a casserole. Cover dish with lid or vented plastic wrap. Microwave on high for 3-4 minutes, stirring once.

Blend cornstarch with water, then stir in ketchup and the next ingredients (salt, pepper, basil, thyme.) Add chicken to vegetables, stir in ketchup mixture. Cover: Microwave at high 7-8 minutes, stirring twice. Serve over pasta or rice. Makes 2-4 servings.

Chicken Fantastico

2-2½ lb of chicken pieces (drumsticks, thighs, legs)
¼ cup all purpose flour
1 tsp salt and pepper
2 tbs vegetable oil
1 cup chopped onions
1 medium green pepper cut into 1-inch pieces
1 clove of garlic, minced
1 1/3 cups of ketchup
1 cup of water
hot cooked rice

Dredge chicken in mixture of flour, salt and pepper. In large skillet, brown chicken in oil. Remove chicken, set aside. In same skillet, sauté onions, green peppers and garlic in drippings until vegetables are tender. Stir any remaining flour mixture into vegetables, and then stir in ketchup and water. Return chicken to skillet. Cover, simmer 35–45 minutes or until chicken is tender, basting occasionally. Skim excess fat from sauce. Serve chicken and sauce with rice. Makes 4-5 servings.

Chicken Meat Loaf

1 pkg chicken or turkey ground meat
½ cup breadcrumbs
1 egg
2 tbs chicken bouillon powder
¼ cup water
1 stalk celery finely chopped
1 clove garlic finely minced

Combine all ingredients in bowl. Mix very well. Place in microwave 5x9 pan. Top with ketchup or tomato sauce. Microwave on high for about 20 minutes. (Varies according to microwave.) Test in the center by slightly pressing fork down. If juices run clear it is cooked. Let stand for about 5 minutes. Slice and serve with mashed potatoes. Or bake for 45 minutes at 350°

Variation

Chicken Meat Balls

Use above recipe and also add Italian seasoning and more garlic. Roll into balls about 1" big. Put them loosely in non-stick skillet with a little oil fry until browned. You may do this in batches depending on size of skillet. Set aside when on paper towel. Place all meatballs in oven proof/microwave proof bowl and add pre-made marinara sauce. Cover and bake or microwave about 15 minutes in microwave or 30 minutes in 350° oven. Test for doneness by cutting one meatball open.

Serve for munchies or over rice or pasta, or in a bun for a late night snack.

Beef Meat Loaf/ Meat Balls

Same recipe as above but omit chicken bouillon and celery and add one package onion soup mix. You can now make meatballs the same as above but with different sauce:

Variation:

Swedish Meat Balls

Meat Loaf recipe
1 can beef bouillon soup
1 container (250 ml) sour cream
2 tbs vegetable oil
1/2 pkg egg noodles cooked

Same recipe as beef meat loaf above but roll into bite size meatballs. Fry in skillet with 2 tbsp of oil until browned. Remove meatballs and place on paper towel. Add bouillon to frying pan. Boil. Stirring well scraping up bits from frying pan. Add sour cream. Add meatballs into sauce. Serve over cooked egg noodles. Serves 2-3.

Meat Ball Sauce:

This is good over rice but not recommended for pasta.

Meatball mixture
1 cup ketchup
1 cup hp sauce

½ cup brown sugar
1 tsp worchester sauce

Mix well. Poor sauce over meatballs and bake according to above recipe. Serve over cooked rice.

Sloppy Joes

A traditional must have

1 tbs vegetable oil
1 lb ground beef
½ cup ketchup
¼ cup loosely packed brown sugar
1 tbs worchester sauce
1 can tomato paste
½ onion diced
4 hamburger buns

In skillet brown meat and onion in vegetable oil, add the rest of the ingredients. Mix well until heated through. Pour over toasted hamburger buns.
Serves 2.

Basic but tasty Pork Chops

The breadcrumbs and searing seals in the juices

2 pork chops

1 cup breadcrumbs seasoned with Italian seasoning, salt, and pepper
1 egg lightly beaten

Season pork chops with salt and pepper, coat with egg, and then coat with breadcrumb seasoning. Brown in skillet both sides with a little oil or non-stick vegetable oil. Bake in 350° oven for 15 minutes.

Creamed Salmon on Toast

1 can inexpensive pink salmon (remove bones, drain)
1 can cream of mushroom soup
¼ cup milk

Combine all ingredients in saucepan and mix well, breaking up the salmon well. Heat through. Serve over toast.
Serves 2.

Tuna Melt

1 can tuna drained
2-3 tbs mayonnaise
1 stalk celery chopped
salt and pepper
1/2 cup grated cheddar cheese
2 english muffins

In bowl combine all ingredients and 1/2 cheese. Heat mixture either in microwave or on stove. Stirring. Toast english muffins. Place tuna mixture on english muffins. Sprinkle with remaining cheese and broil until cheese is bubbly. Serves 2

Chicken Dijon with Mushroom Sauce

2 pieces of skinned chicken
1 can mushroom soup
1 tsp Dijon mustard

In heavy pot add chicken and enough water to cover. Bring to boil and reduce slightly. Add a little salt and poach about 15 minutes or until no longer pink inside. Remove from water and let cool slightly. Dice into bite sized pieces and place in microwave proof casserole dish. Pour soup mixed with mustard over chicken adding a bit of the water from pot to thin out slightly. Microwave 5-7 minutes until bubbly. Top with Parmesan cheese.

Super Easy Mussels

You might think that Mussels are a delicacy and a challenge. On the contrary you can pick up a bag for about $5.00 and have a feast. They are not only cheap, but also very nutritious and you will totally impress your roommates.

1 bag mussels cleaned well

1 clove garlic minced
1 onion chopped
1 can tomatoes with broth
1 tbs Italian seasoning
1 can chicken broth

In a large, heavy pot, heat olive oil and add onion stirring until translucent. Add garlic and stir a bit more. Add chicken broth, tomatoes and seasoning. Bring to a boil breaking up tomatoes. Simmer for about 10 minutes. Bring to boil add mussels coating well. Lower heat to medium high. Cover and cook for about 7-10 minutes or until all the mussels are open, shaking pot frequently. Season to taste. Serve with a baguette for dunking into the wonderful broth or over cooked pasta.

Tip: Mussels that don't close when you tap them, don't cook and mussels that don't open after you cook them don't eat.

These two recipes came from my girlfriend Ruth's web site, News Canada

All New Shepherd's Pie

Just assemble everything in the baking pan, pop in the oven and do your studying while dinner cooks by itself. You don't even have to cook the ground beef first.

1 pkg Hamburger Helper Cheesy Baked Potato Dinner Mix
1 lb lean ground beef

1 pkg frozen mixed vegetables
¼ cup milk

Layer Hamburger Helper potatoes in bottom of 9-inch square baking dish. Crumble uncooked ground beef on top.

Combine Hamburger Helper sauce mix with 2 cups hot water; pour over beef. Layer frozen vegetables over beef. Cover tightly with foil. Bake at 400° for 55-60 minutes.

Baked Enchiladas

Get your friends to help you eat this one up.

1 lb ground beef
1 pkg Old El Paso Soft Taco Kit
1 cup canned or frozen corn
½ cup sweet pepper or zucchini diced
2 cups shredded mozzarella, cheddar, monterey jack or nacho cheese blend
1 can tomato sauce
sour cream (optional)

Brown beef in large skillet over medium-high heat, stirring occasionally. Drain. Stir in 2 cups water and seasoning mix. Cook for 5 minutes. Stir in corn, pepper and 1 cup of the cheese.

Combine taco kit salsa and tomato sauce. Pour 1 cup into 9x13 inch baking dish. Place approximately 1/3 cup beef filling on each taco kit tortilla and roll up. Leaving ends open. Place seam side down in pan.

Pour remaining sauce over tortillas. Sprinkle with remaining cheese. Cover with foil. Bake at 375° for 20-25 minutes. Serve with sour cream if desired.

-News Canada

PASTA

Manicotti with Chicken and Spinach

1 can or jar of marinara pasta sauce
½ pound of ground chicken or turkey meat
½ onion chopped
1 cup spinach chopped, cooked and drained
1 ½ cups cottage cheese
1 tsp dried basil
1 egg
¼ cup parmesan cheese
salt and pepper
8 dried manicotti tubes (microwavable) or fresh lasagne sheets

In frying pan with non-stick cooking spray add chicken or turkey and onion and cook, breaking up meat with spatula until the meat is fully cooked, about 10 minutes. Scrape into a large bowl and let cool for 10 minutes.

Put cooked spinach in a sieve and press against it firmly with the back of a spoon to remove any excess liquid. Add to the meat mixture along with the cottage cheese, basil, egg, parmesan and salt and pepper. Using a spoon beat vigorously to blend.

Preheat oven to 325°. Spread ½ cup of sauce over bottom of baking dish. Add manicotti tubes to boiling water stir well and cook for 8 minutes. They should be *Al dente. Drain and rinse under cold water. With small spoon stuff each tube with 1/3 cup of filling. Arrange in single layer in baking dish and spoon remaining sauce over top. Cover with aluminium foil and bake until sauce is bubbling and the filling is heated through-about 40 minutes. Let stand 5 minutes before serving.

OR

If you are using a microwave, using fresh lasagne noodles cook them until al dente and spoon filling across top portion of noodle and roll into a tube. Arrange accordingly as per above.

Cover with plastic wrap and put in microwave oven for approximately 8-10 minutes until sauce is bubbling and heated through. Let stand 5 minutes before removing wrap.
(Be careful of steam)

*Al Dente-firm not mushy

Mom's Spaghetti and Meat sauce

1 pkg ground beef
1 can tomato sauce
2 tsp Italian Seasoning
1 large can plum tomatoes
1 tsp minced garlic finely chopped
1 onion finely chopped
2 tbs olive oil

2 cups uncooked pasta of your choice

In skillet, brown beef breaking it up into small bits. Remove from pan and drain any oil. Set aside. In same skillet add garlic, onion and olive oil until onions are translucent. Then add tomatoes. Place on low boil breaking up tomatoes as you cook. Add sauce, beef and seasonings. Simmer on low for about 20 minutes. Season to taste. Serve over drained pasta.

Tip: If you are using the regular ground beef, drain it after it has browned before adding other ingredients

Football Night One Pot Spaghetti and Meat Sauce

Cook this on the stove all in one pot

1 tbs cooking oil
1 lb. ground beef or chicken
1 28-ounce can plum tomatoes broken up with juice
1 can sliced mushrooms, with juice
1 can tomato paste
1 ½ cups water
garlic minced
1 cup onion chopped
1 tbs Italian seasoning
pinch sugar
1 tbs hot sauce (optional)
¼ cup grated Parmesan cheese
8 ounces uncooked spaghetti noodles broken in half
Heat oil in large saucepan or Dutch oven add meat and

onion. Scramble-fry until browned and crumbled. Add the rest of ingredients except pasta.

Stir well. Add spaghetti. Make sure all spaghetti is covered with sauce. Cover the pan. Bring to a boil. Reduce heat to medium and boil gently for about 11 minutes until pasta is tender. Sprinkle with extra cheese. Serves 4.

Broccoli Alfredo

1 tbs olive oil
1 can of mushroom soup or cream of chicken soup
1 tsp minced garlic
½ onion chopped
1 cup or a handful of broccoli broken into flowerets*
1 tsp dried Italian seasoning
salt and pepper to taste
½ cup parmesan cheese
4 cups pasta of your choice

Sauté (lightly fry) onions and garlic in oil. Add Italian seasoning, and broccoli and continue to sauté. Add soup and stir well. You may need to add a little milk to dilute. Add cheese and mix well. Season to taste. Pour over cooked pasta.

*Broccoli – break into small bits and place into a bowl with water in it. Cook in the microwave for 2 minutes.

Penne with Tuna Tomato Sauce

1 can tuna drained
1 tsp minced garlic
½ onion finely chopped
1 can tomatoes with liquid
Italian seasoning
salt & pepper to taste
2 cups uncooked penne

Bring large pot ¾ full with water to boil. In the meantime add onion to lightly oiled skillet. Stir and cook until translucent. Add garlic, sauté 1 more minute. Add canned tomatoes and seasoning.

Cook on low boil for about 10 minutes until tomatoes are softened. Add tuna and stir. When water is boiling add pasta. Cook until *Al Dente. Drain and poor into tuna sauce. Stir to combine. Top with Parmesan cheese.

*Al Dente: firm not mushy

Aglio E Olio with Mock Crabmeat

¼ cup olive oil
3 cloves garlic, minced
1 tsp salt
1 pinch hot pepper flakes
½ package mock crabmeat
12 ounces spaghetti

1 tbs Italian seasoning

Fill large pot with water and 2 tablespoons salt; cover and bring to boil. Meanwhile, in skillet, heat oil over low heat; cook garlic add salt and hot pepper flakes, stirring occasionally, for about 3-5 minutes or until garlic is light golden but not browned. Add mock crabmeat to skillet; stir-fry for 2-3 minutes or until warmed through. Meanwhile, add pasta to water, stirring to separate strands. Cook for 8-10 minutes or until tender but firm; drain and return to pot. Add crab and Italian seasoning; toss to coat. Sprinkle parmesan cheese to taste.

Pronto Pasta Primavera

4 cups pasta, your choice
1 cup green pepper sliced
1 cup mushrooms sliced
1 cup onions sliced
½ cup creamy ceasar dressing
1½ cups shredded mozzarella cheese

Cook pasta according to package directions, adding sliced vegetables, during the last 5 minutes of cooking; drain and return to pot. Stir in dressing to coat pasta. Toss in shredded cheese and serve. Serves 2-4

Beefaroni

1 lb ground beef
1 can tomato sauce
1 tbs soya sauce
¼ cup grated cheddar cheese
2 cups cooked penne or macaroni
hot sauce (optional)

If you are limited to the number of pots you have. Cook the pasta first drain and set aside. Then in that pot brown meat add tomato sauce and mix in cooked pasta. Stir on low heat. Heat through. Add cheddar cheese. Mix through. Season to taste.

No-cook Summer Pasta Sauce

3 large plum tomatoes chopped
1 clove of garlic minced
1/2 of an onion chopped
Italian seasoning
1/4 cup olive oil
2 tbs balsamic vinegar
salt and pepper

Combine all ingredients. Let rest for 1/2 hour. Can refrigerate overnight. Toss with cooked angel hair pasta garnish with parmesan.

Pizza Muffins

english muffins
mozzarella cheese
tomato paste
salami (optional)

Toast muffins. Spread tomato paste on muffins. Top with meat and then cheese. Broil until cheese bubbles.

VEGETABLES

Green Beans with Garlic

1 lb of green beans
olive oil
clove of garlic, minced
Italian seasoning
salt and pepper to taste

In a large saucepan, cook beans until barely tender. Drain and immerse in cold water. In saucepan add garlic, oil, beans and oregano. Toss and cook. Taste and adjust, serve immediately.

Crammin' Carrots

Carrots are cheap and easy to store. You can keep them in your fridge for quite a while and are high in vitamins and carotene for better eyesight.

2 carrots peeled and sliced into chunks
1 tbs brown sugar
1 tbs butter

In saucepan cover carrots with water and bring to boil. Cook about 8 minutes until tender. Drain. Add sugar and butter. Toss to coat until butter is melted. Serve at once. Serves 1-2

Asian Stir-fry Veggies

You can use 2 cups of frozen Asian style veggies or fresh.

½ cup broccoli chopped
2 carrots thinly sliced
1 onion thinly sliced
½ green pepper
½ red pepper
2 tsp chicken bouillon powder
¼ cup soya sauce
1 tbs brown sugar

In a skillet add oil for sautéing. Add all vegetables and sauté until onions are translucent. If you want the vegetables softer add a bit of water and put the lid on. Steam for about 3-5 minutes depending on your desired tenderness. Add the rest of the ingredients and sauté. Adjust seasoning and serve over rice.

Tip: If you have leftover rice just add it in at the end to heat it all through. No need for another pot.

POTATOES AND RICE

Rice

You can use the instant rice, but Converted rice is best and quite frankly cheaper.

1 cup converted rice
2 cups water

Put water in a rather small saucepan. Add rice and bring to boil. When it comes to a boil reduce heat to simmer and put lid on for 20 minutes. Don't peek! It will be perfect. Remove from heat and fluff with fork.

Tip: Make double the recipe 2-1 portions and you can make awesome fried rice the next day

Chinese Fried Rice

2 cups of cold cooked rice
¼ cup soya sauce
1 green onion chopped
1 egg slightly beaten with a fork

canned or frozen peas, drained
vegetable oil
1 cup of celery, chopped

In a wok or a large skillet add onion to oil. Sauté and add cold rice and soya sauce. Stir and blend well. In the middle of the skillet make a well. Crack the egg in the middle. As it starts to cook, fork it into the rice to blend. Add the vegetables. Season to taste.

Easy Home Fries

1 can sliced potatoes
½ onion chopped
1 tbs paprika
1 tsp chicken bouillon powder
1 tbs margarine or butter
pepper to taste

In frying pan sauté onion in butter until onions are translucent. Add drained potatoes and sauté until heated through 2-3 minutes. Add paprika and bouillon powder. Stir well. Taste and adjust seasoning.

Tip: canned potatoes and chicken bouillon are salty so no need to add any more salt.

Greasy Spoon Home Fries

2 cooked potatoes with skin – cold
1 tbs chicken powder
2 tsp paprika
salt and pepper to taste
1 onion chopped
3 tbs butter or margarine
1 tbs vegetable oil

Remove skin from one potato. Chop it and add to a medium heat pan with butter and onion. Chop other potato and add it to the pan. Add chicken powder, paprika, salt and pepper. You may need to add more butter.

Tip: adding a little oil to the butter prevents the butter from burning

Easy and Awesome French Fries

2 large baking potatoes washed and very well dried

2 cups vegetable oil

Slice potatoes into thin wedges. (If too thick they will take too long to cook). Add oil into heavy pot and put on high heat. When bubbles start add one potato to test. If oil sizzles heavily the oil is ready. With slotted spoon (if you have one) add a handful of potato slices and make sure they are not sticking together. If boiling too much turn heat down slightly. After about 3 minutes take one out and taste for doneness. If cooked remove them all with slotted spoon and drain on paper towel. Immediately add salt. Repeat process until all are cooked.

Baked French Fries

Instead of cooking potatoes in hot oil toss the sliced potatoes and about ¼ cup of oil in a bowl and spread them on baking sheet. Sprinkle with salt and bake at 375° until tender, about 15 minutes.

Fun stuff to add

Chili Fries

Heat a can of chili and poor over fries to make chili fries.

Poutine

1/2 can beef gravy mix heated
1/2 cup mozzarella sliced thinly or grated if you have a grater
Put half the fries in a bowl. Poor hot gravy and cheese

over top. Repeat process and microwave for about 30 seconds to melt cheese a bit more. *Don't over microwave or the fries will be soggy.

Sweet Potato Fries

Healthy and easy

2 sweet potatoes peeled and sliced into fries or wedges
2 tsp chicken bouillon
seasoning salt (or just salt if you don't have any)
pepper
cajun spice (optional)
3 tbs olive oil

Heat oven to 375° and slice potatoes. Spread on cookie sheet and season with chicken bouillon powder, salt and pepper. Spread oil over potatoes and shake to coat all potatoes. Bake for about 30 minutes or until cooked. Season again if needed.

Mashed Potatoes

(If you don't have a potato masher use your fork or even a mix master)

2 large russet potatoes peeled, washed and cut into cubes
2 tbs butter or margarine
¼ cup hot milk
Bring heavy pot of water to boil
Add potatoes and a pinch of salt

Cook for about 20 minutes or until tender. Drain. Put back in pot and add about 2 tablespoons of butter or margarine and about ¼ cup hot milk. Mash with potato masher or mix with beater. If you don't have either just mash with fork as best you can. Season to taste.

Tip: The trick to making them fluffy is the hot milk.

DESSERTS

Microwave Chocolate Pudding Cake

This is so easy and very decadent

8 oz package chocolate chips
1 ½ cups Bisquick
½ cup of nuts (optional)
1/3 cup sugar
1 ½ cups hot water
½ cup milk
2 tbs vegetable oil
1 tsp vanilla
1 egg
2/3 cup sugar

Put 1/3 cup chocolate chips in microwave on high 1-3 minutes. Mix in Bisquick, nuts, 1/3 cup sugar, milk, oil, vanilla, egg. Stir vigorously with fork. In another bowl add hot water, 2/3 cup sugar, the rest of the chocolate chips. Cook on high for 2 minutes. Stir. Cook for another 2-4 minutes until boiling. Pour this mixture over the first casserole. Cook on medium for 9 minutes. Turn. Cook on high for 5-7 minutes until dry on top.

(Microwave times may vary. Serve with whip cream or ice cream. Warm or cold.)

Rum Balls

2-3 cups graham cracker crumbs
2 tbs cocoa plus more for garnish
¼ cup rum
1 can condensed milk

In large bowl add all ingredients and mix well. Mixture should be easy to roll in the palm of your hand. If too loose add more graham cracker crumbs. Roll in palm of you hand and set aside. When completed roll them in either graham cracker crumbs or cocoa and refrigerate for about 2 hours.

Peanut Butter Fudge

1/3 cup milk
1 package (serves 6) butterscotch pudding
3 tbsp butter
½ cup crunchy peanut butter
2 ½ cups icing sugar

Line loft pan with waxed paper. Blend milk gradually into pudding mix. Add butter and half the peanut butter. Microwave for 50 seconds. Mixture should just start to boil around the edges. Stir well, quickly blend icing sugar in 3 parts. Pour into pan. Melt remaining peanut butter in microwave on high for 20 seconds. Pour over fudge. Chill for 45 minutes – 1 hour.

Christmas Yule Log

Don't wait for Christmas to enjoy this easy desert.

1 pkg chocolate wafers
1 cup whipping cream whipped with 1 tbs sugar to taste,
or 1 can of pre-whipped cream.

*Tip: you can buy the can of pre-whipped- don't add sugar
to that. Make sure it is the real whipped cream, not the
edible oil product.*

Spread wafers with whipped cream and layer together to
form a log. Refrigerate overnight. Cut on the diagonal.

Peanut Butter Cookies

definitely a midnight munchie recipe

1 egg
1 cup peanut butter
1/2 cup sugar

Combine all ingredients. Roll into balls in your hand or
drop them from a spoon and place on ungreased cookie sheet.
Bake in oven at 350° for 15-18 minutes. Let cool completely.

Tip: even better frozen.

Rice Crispy Squares

6 cups rice cereal
¼ cup butter or margarine
35 large marshmallows

Melt butter and marshmallows in saucepan on medium heat, stirring often until melted. Add cereal and stir well. Grease pan poor cereal into greased 9x9 pan. Press down and chill for about 2 hours before cutting.

Quick Brown Sugar Fudge

My mom made this for us when we were vacationing in Barbados. Although she used the local Demerara sugar, brown sugar will do the trick. She made it in our kitchenette motel room. If she can do it there you can pull it off too. It takes care of your sweet cravings.

1 cup packed brown sugar
2 tbs margarine
1 tbs milk

In saucepan combine all ingredients on high heat. Stirring constantly until mixture comes to a rolling boil. Cook about 2 minutes then remove from heat and whisk with a fork or whisker for about 5 minutes. It will give you a workout but worth it. When the fudge is a shiny and smooth consistency poor onto plate or pan coated with non-stick cooking spray or a little margarine. Allow to cool in fridge about 1 hour.

www.ingramcontent.com/pod-product-compliance
Lightning Source LLC
Chambersburg PA
CBHW071645040426
42452CB00009B/1773